STEM *trailblazer* BIOS

ALTERNATE REALITY
GAME DESIGNER
JANE MCGONIGAL

ANASTASIA SUEN

Lerner Publications Company
Minneapolis

Lerner Publications Company
A division of Lerner Publishing Group, Inc.
241 First Avenue North
Minneapolis, MN 55401 U.S.A.

For reading levels and more information, look up this title at www.lernerbooks.com.

Content Consultant: Lee Sheldon, Associate Professor, Department of Communication and Media, Games and Simulation Arts and Sciences, Rensselaer Polytechnic Institute

The Cataloging-in-Publication Data for *Alternate Reality Game Designer Jane McGonigal* is on file at the Library of Congress.
    ISBN 978–1–4677–2458–6 (library binding : alkaline paper)
    ISBN 978–1–4677–2488–3 (eBook)

Manufactured in the United States of America
1 – PC – 12/31/13

The images in this book are used with the permission of; © Evan Amos/Wikimedia Commons, p. 4; © Brian Snyder/Reuters/Newscom, pp. 5, 26; © Red Line Editorial, pp. 7, 8, 10, 18; © Alison Yin/AP Images, p. 11; © Erika Cross/Shutterstock Images, p. 12; © Songquan Deng/Shutterstock Images, p. 13; © Ambient Images Inc./SuperStock, p. 14; © Marc Bryan-Brown/Getty Images, p. 15; © Thinkstock, p. 17; © Gregory Urquiaga/MCT/Newscom, p. 20; © Luna Vandoorne/Shutterstock Images, p. 23; © Mindy Best/Getty Images, pp. 25, 27.

Front cover: © Gabriela Hasbun/Aurora Photos/Alamy.

Main body text set in Adrianna Regular 13/22. Typeface provided by Chank.

CONTENTS

Chapter 1

The Atari 2600 was one of the earliest home video game systems.

GROWING UP
WITH GAMES

In the world of video games, October 1977 was an important time. The first Atari 2600 home video game **console** came out that month. The Atari hooked up to a TV, and players could choose from nine different games. Each

game was stored on a cartridge, a hard case with software inside. Players put a cartridge into the Atari console to play a game. People liked that they no longer had to go to an arcade to play video games. The Atari was a huge hit.

Another event happened in October 1977 that would change video game history: Jane McGonigal was born. Jane would grow up to change the way people played and thought of games.

Jane McGonigal has spent her life playing and creating games.

TECH TALK

"When I was in fifth grade, we got our first home computer. It was a Commodore 64. . . . One of the games we got was a game called *Load Runner*. I instantly became obsessed with that and I would fall asleep at night dreaming in *Load Runner* and wake up with new ideas for levels. So I learned some basic programming and started making games."

—*Jane McGonigal*

FAMILY TIME

Jane grew up in Moorestown, New Jersey. Both of her parents were schoolteachers. When Jane was young, she played games at home with her family. She liked to play *KC Munchkin* with her twin sister, Kelly, and her dad. It was an arcade-style video game similar to *Pac-Man*. Jane's family played on a Magnavox Odyssey 2 game console in the living room.

After her family bought a computer, Jane started writing her own games. She created games for her sister and her mom. Jane's favorite books, the Choose Your Own Adventure series, inspired her. She started writing her own computer code—a set of instructions for a program—to make games. Jane designed all the art for her games using the letters, numbers, and symbols on her computer keyboard. One of her games was called *You Be the Judge*. It featured a giant cat. She designed a cat to be the main character because it was easier to draw with the computer keys than a human was.

KC Munchkin (below) was an arcade-style video game similar to *Pac-Man*.

```
YOU DROVE WEST FROM LONDON ALL DAY IN
YOUR NEW LITTLE BRITISH SPORTS CAR. NOW
AT LAST YOU'VE ARRIVED IN THE STORIED
LAND OF CORNWALL.

DUSK HAS FALLEN AS YOU PULL UP IN FRONT
OF TRESYLLIAN CASTLE. A GHOSTLY FULL
MOON IS RISING, AND A TALL IRON GATE
BETWEEN TWO PILLARS BARS THE WAY INTO
THE COURTYARD.

WHAT WOULD YOU LIKE TO DO?
>※
```

Text adventure games such as *Moonmist* looked very different from today's advanced, colorful video games.

GAME ADVENTURES

When Jane wasn't making games, she was playing them. She loved the Infocom text adventures series. The games didn't have any pictures—only stories filled with puzzles. To play the game, Jane had to solve the mysteries.

TECH TALK

"To me, computers and video games have always been a way to bond with my family, to express myself, and to become smarter and more interesting. Games have always been a way to have real adventures with friends that would forever shape our relationships to each other, adventures that I would remember for the rest of my life."

—Jane McGonigal

MOONMIST

When Jane was in seventh grade, her friend Junior helped her beat a game. He had solved *Moonmist,* Jane's favorite text adventure game. He gave Jane a paper with the **solution**. It told her what steps to take to win the game. Jane had been trying to solve that murder mystery game for two years. Now she knew exactly what to do. Jane was so happy to finally beat *Moonmist.* She saved that paper for years!

WORKING TOGETHER

The summer after Jane and her sister graduated from high school, they found out that the most popular girl in their class

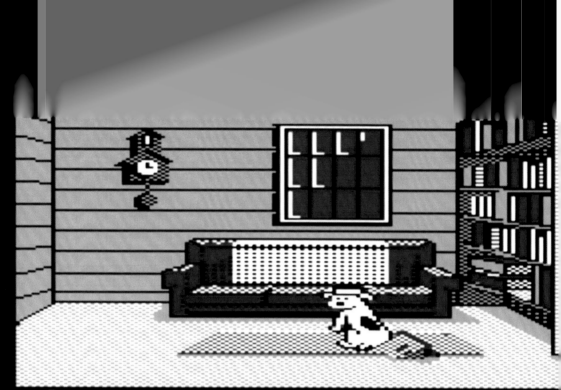

Press any key to start the game.

Jane, her twin sister, Kelly, and their new friend were determined to beat *Tass Times in Tonetown.*

liked to play games too. Jane and Kelly spent the summer in their new friend's basement. The three of them played *Tass Times in Tonetown* on an old computer.

The goal of the game was to find a book and deliver it to a character called Gramps. To deliver the book and win, they had to travel to many places in the game. The girls had never won the game before. They decided to play it together and finish the game once and for all. Just before they left for college, they finally beat the game! They treated themselves to frozen yogurt to celebrate.

McGonigal talks about games with Jack Tretton, Sony Computer Entertainment CEO, in 2011.

McGonigal studied English and was the news editor for Fordham's school newspaper.

A NEW ADVENTURE

McGonigal went to college at Fordham College in New York City. Even in college, McGonigal still played games. During her senior year, she worked for the New York City Department of Parks and Recreation. She was in charge of the games people played at outdoor festivals in Central Park. Hundreds of people came together in Central Park to run and jump and play sports.

McGonigal graduated from college in 1999 after a fun summer of outdoor games. She started working as a writer and an editor during the day. At night, she worked in a theater. She worked behind the scenes as a stage manager.

For the Parks Department, McGonigal coordinated physical games for people to play outside in Central Park.

Chapter 3

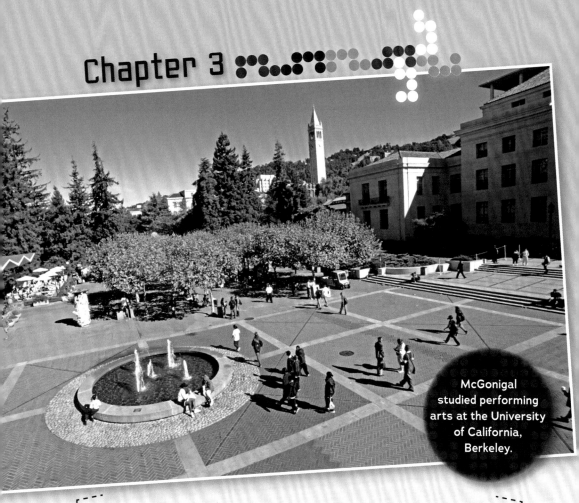

McGonigal studied performing arts at the University of California, Berkeley.

ALTERNATE REALITY GAMES

In 2001, McGonigal decided to go back to college. She moved across the country to go to school at the University of California, Berkeley. While she was at school, McGonigal worked for the Go Game. It was similar to her job with the

Parks Department in New York City. But the Go Game made games that took place all over the city. These games included puzzles to solve and missions to complete.

In some ways, McGonigal's new job was like her job in the theater. As a stage manager, McGonigal took care of actors, sets, and props. For the Go Game, she was doing that for a different stage—an alternate reality game (ARG). An ARG uses the real world as its stage. ARGs can happen anywhere.

As a game designer, McGonigal gets to decide where players go and what they do to play the game.

INS AND OUTS OF ARGS

An ARG is like a reality TV show. The shows *Survivor* and *The Amazing Race* are games that take place in the real world. Like these TV game shows, players in ARGs follow clues. They work together in real life to solve a problem. In some ARGs, the players meet one another. This happens when the game is played in one place. But some games take place all around the world. In these games, the players meet one another online.

Behind every game is a story. To live out the story, players solve puzzles, follow clues, and go on missions created by the designer. Clues can be found in sound recordings, video, or printed words. These clues can be hidden in real places or

Because ARGs take place in the real world, clues can come in different forms, such as a text message or a phone call from a pay phone.

online. To find game clues, players visit web pages and blogs. They read e-mail and text messages on their phones.

An ARG can take days, weeks, or months to play. To solve the clues, players have to work together. They go on missions and perform tasks. They have to follow the game's story. It is the game designer's job to create this world. When designing ARGs, McGonigal invents imaginary characters and situations. She creates a story for the games and thinks of problems and puzzles for the players to solve.

www.ilovebees.com

Margaret's Honey
napa valley, ca

home   about me   the hives

They
they
hey make
Couldn't
somethin
be

HALT – MODULE CORE HEMOF

Control has been yielded
SYSTEM PERIL DISTRIBUTED

grope:
seeker > lottoch Princess
foil ᵗmsg: SPDR-5.14.3

evade evade evade

!probe extern proc 1
rogue proc

!bite rogue proc 1 recurse
clean !splotch confidence 100

Mission Log   MIA   Rec

COUNTDOWN TO WIDE AWAKE AND
196966:15:22:33:55

Make your decisions accor

The website for the game *I Love Bees* looked like a site about beekeeping at first. But then a message popped up showing that it was a game.

I LOVE BEES

In 2004, McGonigal started working for 42 Entertainment while she was still in school. The company designed ARGs. Microsoft asked 42 Entertainment to make an ARG to promote Microsoft's new Xbox game called *Halo 2*. McGonigal created the game *I Love Bees*. The web address for the game appeared at the end of a *Halo 2* trailer. People started visiting the page. As the website loaded, it looked like a beekeeper's page. Then it changed. Some of the page did not make sense. A note at the bottom asked for help. After that, a number puzzle and a clock showed up.

More than six hundred thousand people worked on this puzzle. Together, they figured out that the numbers were locations and times. They figured out that the clock would run out on a certain day. On that day, people showed up at the time listed for each site. At each location, a pay phone rang. A voice on the phone asked a question. That led to more clues. For four months, new clues appeared. To solve the puzzle, the players had to work together. McGonigal's new game was a huge hit! Other game developers were impressed too. McGonigal's team won the International Game Developers Association's Innovation Award for *I Love Bees* in 2005.

Teaching and making games became McGonigal's full-time job.

DESIGNING GAMES

McGonigal had gone to UC Berkeley to study theater. But after she discovered ARGs, she wanted to change studies. She convinced the school to let her study games. Part of her studies included finding new ways to play games and learning how people played them. No one had ever studied it at the college level before. She earned a doctorate, the highest level of college degree, in 2006. While she was still a student, McGonigal taught game design and game **theory** at UC Berkeley. She also taught at the San Francisco Art Institute.

IDEAS FOR NEW GAMES

McGonigal got ideas for new games from what was happening in the world. In 2007, the price of oil went up as demand for oil grew. More people around the world were using oil. People wondered what would happen if it ran out. McGonigal wanted people to think of ways to live with less oil. With the help of a team, she created *World Without Oil.* This ARG was also a **simulation** game. In simulation games, players solve problems that can happen in real life. In *World Without Oil*, players had to survive an imaginary oil shortage. For six weeks, players around the globe came up with solutions. They worked together in the game to solve a real-world problem.

THE LOST RING

McGonigal also created an ARG for the 2008 Summer Olympics. It was called *The Lost Ring.* The game began in February when packages arrived at people's doorsteps. Inside

ARGs FOR COMPANIES

Different companies have asked McGonigal to make ARGs for their employees. She has led teams that made games for Intel, Nike, Disney, McDonald's, Microsoft, and Nintendo. In these ARGs, workers played together to overcome challenges. Learning how to play ARGs as a team helps them work together at their jobs.

were clues, such as messages and photographs. Then videos could be found online. In them, five athletes reappeared from two thousand years ago. Athletes knew they had a mission to complete, but they weren't sure what it was. Clues to what the lost ring was were found around the world. The players who found them communicated online. They created web pages to save the clues in one place.

It took months to figure out what the lost ring was. It turned out to be a lost Olympic sport with a maze that went in a circle. New teams formed all over the world to re-create the sport. Players made chalk circles on the ground. Then they

Blindfolds played an important role in the ARG called *The Lost Ring*.

blindfolded one player. That person ran inside the circle. The others made the walls of the maze with their bodies. They hummed so the blindfolded person knew where to go next.

The teams posted videos of their maze running online. They practiced for their own Lost Sport Olympics, which took place during the 2008 Olympics in Beijing. On August 23 and 24, teams on six continents raced in the Lost Sport Olympics. Approximately 5,000 people played the game, and more than 2.5 million people worldwide watched it online!

HELPING OTHERS

In 2009, as McGonigal was picking up some papers in her office, she hit her head on a cabinet. She got a **concussion** and was dizzy and sick for three months. McGonigal was upset that she wasn't getting better. She decided to make her recovery into a game she called *SuperBetter*.

McGonigal asked her family and friends to call her every day. She wanted them to give her small tasks to complete. They asked her to look out the window or take a short walk. Accomplishing tasks helped McGonigal start to feel better. Her family and friends were there to give her new goals and cheer her on. With their help, Jane got well.

Now *SuperBetter* is an ARG that others can play too. McGonigal designed it to help players build up four different kinds of strength: mental, physical, emotional, and social. The goal is for players to use their strengths to face

McGonigal gives a speech titled "A Crash Course in Becoming SuperBetter" at a music and film festival in 2012.

In 2011, McGonigal spoke about her book and her thoughts on games at a gaming conference in Boston, Massachusetts.

real-life challenges. It can be played on the web, or it can be downloaded to a smartphone.

After McGonigal got better, she went back to work writing a book she had started before her concussion. She wrote about *SuperBetter* in her book, titled *Reality Is Broken: Why Games Make Us Better and How They Can Change the World.* In it, she also wrote about how games can help us solve real-world problems every day. The book hit stores in 2011 and became a *New York Times* best seller.

THE FUTURE OF GAMING

McGonigal sees a future in which everyone plays games. She travels around the world talking about how games help people work together. In 2013, McGonigal spoke at a conference of

McGonigal signs copies of her book, *Reality Is Broken: Why Games Make Us Better and How They Can Change the World.*

TECH TALK

"Games have shown us our own potential for happiness, change, and success. I believe games can make all of us happier in our real lives, not just in virtual environments. I believe as gamers, we can do more than save virtual worlds—we can help save the real world."

—Jane McGonigal

the International Society for Technology in Education. She told teachers there that playing games teaches important skills. McGonigal believes that people who play games learn how to work together. They don't get upset and give up. They believe in themselves and keep trying.

McGonigal says teachers, doctors, scientists, and the government could all use games to solve problems. And she suggests that gamers spend 10 percent of their game time on ARGs. By working together, she believes that game players could solve the world's real problems. For McGonigal, designing and playing games is a way for the world to face its toughest challenges.

TIMELINE

1977

Jane McGonigal is born in Philadelphia, Pennsylvania, in October.

1999

McGonigal graduates from Fordham College in New York City with a degree in English.

2001

McGonigal moves to California to attend the University of California, Berkeley, and begins playing ARGs.

2005

McGonigal's ARG *I Love Bees* wins the 2005 International Game Developers Association's Innovation Award.

2006

McGonigal graduates from the University of California, Berkeley, with a doctorate degree. She teaches game design and game theory.

2007

McGonigal creates *World Without Oil*.

2008

More than 2.5 million people watch the Lost Sport Olympics, the finale to McGonigal's game *The Lost Ring*, online.

2011

McGonigal's book *Reality Is Broken: Why Games Make Us Better and How They Can Change the World* becomes a *New York Times* best seller.

2013

McGonigal is the keynote speaker at the International Society for Technology in Education annual conference.

GLOSSARY

concussion
an injury to the brain caused by a heavy blow to the head

console
an electronic device for playing video games

simulation
the act of imitating a behavior or situation

solution
the answer to a problem

theory
the rules of an art or a practice

virtual
existing on a computer or online

SOURCE NOTES

6 Sanjay Gupta, "Interview with Video Game Guru Jane McGonigal," *CNN*, April 15, 2012, accessed July 11, 2013, http://transcripts.cnn.com/TRANSCRIPTS/1204/15/nl.01.html.

9 Jane McGonigal, "Growing Up Gamer," accessed July 10, 2013, http://www.avantgame.com_growing_up_gamer_mcgonigal_sept2008.pdf.

16 Gupta, "Interview with Video Game Guru Jane McGonigal."

28 McGonigal, "Growing Up Gamer."

FURTHER INFORMATION

BOOKS

Guinness World Records. *Guinness World Records 2013 Gamer's Edition*. New York: Guinness World Records, 2013. Check out this book for gaming records, trivia, and all the latest news in the gaming world.

Harbour, Jonathan S. *Video Game Programming for Kids*. Boston: Cengage Learning, 2012. This book teaches programming through simple concepts and example games.

Kaplan, Arie. *The Epic Evolution of Video Games*. Minneapolis: Lerner Publications, 2014. Take a closer look at how video games have changed over time and what future games might be like.

WEBSITES

JaneMcGonigal.com
http://janemcgonigal.com/play-me
Watch trailers for many of Jane McGonigal's ARGs, and read more about why she creates them.

TED: Jane McGonigal: Gaming Can Make a Better World
http://www.ted.com/talks/jane_mcgonigal_gaming_can_make_a_better_world.html
Hear why McGonigal thinks it's important for more people to play ARGs.

World Without Oil
http://worldwithoutoil.org
Watch the *World Without Oil* game trailer, and learn all about the game.

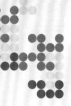

INDEX

ABOUT THE AUTHOR

Anastasia Suen has taught kindergarten to college. The prolific author of more than 160 books and the founder of STEM Friday, she writes about science, technology, engineering, and mathematics for children, teens, and adults. Suen lives with her family in Plano, Texas.